Foreword

Your Graces

It is clear from the use which has been made of *Holy Communion: Series 2* both at home and abroad during the past four years that the rite has served a useful purpose. It has been a valuable means of experiment at home, while its influence on the new rites of other Churches has been far from negligible. Nevertheless, it was never intended to be a finished product; and experience has revealed its limitations. We believed that it was simply a step in the right direction. That belief has been justified: for we have been able to build Series 3 on the foundations of Series 2; and although there are all kinds of changes in language and detail, we have found no solid reason to make any serious departure from the basic structure of our original rite. It is a matter of great pleasure to us to be able to present a unanimous Report. We have succeeded in overcoming the problems which divided us in 1966, and here we must express our deep gratitude to those many people who have helped us and in particular to our friends of the Doctrine Commission. We hope that the Church of England will find in this rite a further significant step towards the creation of a new and worthy Book of Common Prayer in the not too distant future.

R C D Jasper
June 1971

D0234267

1

Members of the Commission

The Reverend Canon R C D Jasper, MA, DD, FRHistS
Chairman

The Bishop of Newcastle
The Right Reverend H E Ashdown DD

The Provost of Derby
The Very Reverend R A Beddoes MA

The Bishop of Derby
The Right Reverend C W J Bowles MA

The Reverend C O Buchanan MA

The Reverend Canon G J Cuming MA, DD

Mr D L Frost MA, PhD

The Reverend D C Gray TD, AKC

The Dean of Bristol
The Very Reverend D E W Harrison MA, DLitt
Vice-Chairman

Mr T S Horan

The Reverend J L Houlden MA

Mrs J M Mayland MA, DipTh

Mrs E M Montefiore MA

The Reverend Canon P C Moore MA, DPhil

The Reverend L E H Stephens-Hodge MA

The Reverend Canon C V Taylor MA

The Reverend Canon E C Whitaker MA

Miss M D Fraser BA, MTh
Secretary

Corresponding Members:

The Bishop of St Edmundsbury and Ipswich
The Right Reverend L W Brown DD

Mr Alan Wicks MusBac, FRCO

The Reverend J D Wilkinson MA

Notes

1 **Posture.** Wherever a certain posture is particularly appropriate, it is indicated in the left-hand margin. At all other points local custom may be established and followed.

2 **Saying and singing.** Where rubrics indicate that a section is to be 'said', this must be understood to include 'or sung' and vice versa.

3 **Seasonal material.** The proper thanksgivings (28) are obligatory; but the seasonal sentences (1, 37) and the seasonal blessings (44) are optional. The use of one portion of the optional material does not necessitate the use of the other portions.

4 **Series 2 material.** During the initial period of experiment, it is permitted to use in certain sections the texts prescribed in Holy Communion Series 2 instead of the texts printed here. These sections are: the Salutation (3), the Collect for Purity (4), the Gloria in Excelsis (5), the responses to the Gospel (11), the Nicene Creed (13), the Prayers (15), the Comfortable Words (17), the Confession (18), the Prayer of Humble Access (20), the Lord's Prayer (31), the Anthems (34), and the final prayer after communion (39). Where parts of the service are also sung to well-known musical settings, it is also permitted to use the words for which these settings were composed.

5 **The Kyries (5).** The Kyries may be said or sung in English or Greek. In penitential seasons it is desirable

that this section should be used in preference to Gloria in Excelsis.

6 The Gloria in Excelsis (5). This canticle is also appropriate at sections 2, 10, or 40.

7 The Collects (6). The Collects are either those appointed in the Book of Common Prayer or those appended to Holy Communion Series 1.

8 The Lessons (7, 9, 11). The Lessons should be announced in the order: book, chapter, verse. They should be either those set out in Tables 1–3 appended to Holy Communion Series 3, or those in the Book of Common Prayer, or any other lessons which are authorized for use in the Church of England. When the lessons of Table 1 appended to Series 3 are used and only two lessons are read, the Epistle should be omitted during Advent and the last five weeks of Trinity; the Old Testament lesson should be omitted during the rest of Trinity and Whitsun; and either the Old Testament lesson or the Epistle may be omitted from Christmas until the end of Easter.

9 The Sermon (12). A sermon should be preached at (12) whenever possible; but it is not necessary at every service.

10 The Prayers (15). The introduction to the specific subjects of prayer is not restricted to the printed forms 'we give thanks for', 'we pray for', 'we commemorate'. Other forms may be used at the discretion of the minister provided they are clearly addressed to God.

11 The Peace (22). The president may accompany the words of the Peace with a handclasp or similar action: and both the words and the action may be passed through the congregation.

12 The Thanksgiving (26-29). During the Thanksgiving the president may be joined by any other priests who are present.

13 A Service without Communion. When there is to be no communion, the minister reads the service as far as the absolution (19) and then adds the Lord's Prayer (31), the General Thanksgiving, and other prayers at his discretion, ending with the Grace. When such a service is led by a deacon or lay person, 'us' is said instead of 'you' in the Absolution (19).

14 Hymns. Various points are indicated for the singing of hymns; but if occasion requires they may be sung at other points also.

Seasonal Sentences

Advent The glory of the Lord shall be revealed, and all mankind shall see it.

Christmas I bring you news of great joy, a joy to be shared by the whole people. Today in the town of David a saviour has been born to you; he is Christ the Lord.

Epiphany The grace of God has dawned upon the world with healing for all mankind.

Lent Compassion and forgiveness belong to the Lord our God, though we have rebelled against him.

Passiontide Christ himself bore our sins in his body on the tree, that we might die to sin and live to righteousness. By his wounds you have been healed.

Easter It is true: the Lord has risen: alleluia!

Ascension Christ has gone up on high: alleluia!

Whitsun God's love has been shed abroad in our hearts through the Holy Spirit he has given us.

Trinity Sunday By day and by night around the throne they sing: Holy, holy, holy is God the sovereign Lord of all; he was, he is, and he is to come.

Saints' Days	Since we are surrounded by so great a cloud of witnesses, let us lay aside every weight, and sin which clings so closely, and let us run with perseverance the race that is set before us.
Harvest	The earth is the Lord's and all that is in it.
Dedication	Truly the Lord is in this place; this is no other than the house of God; this is the gate of heaven.
Unity	How good and pleasant it is when brothers live together in unity!

The Word and The Prayers

The Preparation

2 At the entry of the ministers a hymn, a canticle, or a psalm may be sung, and a sentence (pp. 7–8) may be used.

3 The minister may say

> The Lord be with you.

All **And also with you.**

4 **All** **Almighty God,**
to whom all hearts are open,
all desires known,
and from whom no secrets are hid:
cleanse the thoughts of our hearts
by the inspiration of your Holy Spirit,
that we may perfectly love you,
and worthily magnify your holy Name;
through Christ our Lord. Amen.

5 The Kyries may be said.

> Lord, have mercy.
> **Lord, have mercy.**
> Lord, have mercy.
>
> **Christ, have mercy.**
> Christ, have mercy.
> **Christ, have mercy.**
>
> Lord, have mercy.
> **Lord, have mercy.**
> Lord, have mercy.

Or the canticle Gloria in Excelsis may be said.

All   **Glory to God in the highest,**
and peace to his people on earth.

Lord God, heavenly King,
almighty God and Father,
we worship you, we give you thanks,
we praise you for your glory.

Lord Jesus Christ, only Son of the Father,
Lord God, Lamb of God,
you take away the sin of the world:
have mercy on us;
you are seated at the right hand of the
    Father:
receive our prayer.

For you alone are the Holy One,
you alone are the Lord,
you alone are the Most High,
Jesus Christ, with the Holy Spirit,
in the glory of God the Father. Amen.

6   The collect of the day.

The Ministry of the Word

7 Sit
The Old Testament lesson. At the end the reader says

> This is the word of the Lord.

Silence may be kept.

8 A psalm may be said.

9 The Epistle. At the end the reader says

> This is the word of the Lord.

Silence may be kept.

10 A canticle, a hymn, or a psalm may be sung.

11 Stand
The Gospel. When it is announced

All **Glory to Christ our Saviour.**

At the end the reader says

> This is the Gospel of Christ.

All **Praise to Christ our Lord.**

Silence may be kept.

12 Sit
The sermon.

At the end silence may be kept.

13 Stand

The Nicene Creed is said, at least on Sundays and
greater Holy Days.

All   **We believe in one God,
the Father, the Almighty,
maker of heaven and earth,
of all that is seen and unseen.**

      **We believe in one Lord, Jesus Christ,
the only Son of God,
eternally begotten of the Father,
God from God, Light from Light,
true God from true God,
begotten, not made,
one in Being with the Father.
Through him all things were made.
For us men and for our salvation
he came down from heaven;
by the power of the Holy Spirit
he was born of the Virgin Mary,
and became man.
For our sake he was crucified under
Pontius Pilate;
he suffered, died, and was buried.
On the third day he rose again
in fulfilment of the Scriptures;
he ascended into heaven
and is seated at the right hand of the
Father.
He will come again in glory
to judge the living and the dead,
and his kingdom will have no end.**

**We believe in the Holy Spirit, the Lord,
the giver of life,
who proceeds from the Father and the
Son.
With the Father and the Son he is
worshipped and glorified.
He has spoken through the Prophets.
We believe in one holy catholic and
apostolic Church.
We acknowledge one baptism for the
forgiveness of sins.
We look for the resurrection of the dead,
and the life of the world to come. Amen.**

The Prayers

14 Banns of marriage and other notices may be published;
the offerings of the people may be collected; and a
hymn may be sung.

15 Intercessions and thanksgivings are offered by the
president or by some other person.
It is not necessary to include specific subjects in any
section of the following prayer.
The set passages may also follow one another as a con-
tinuous whole, without the versicles and responses.

Minister Let us pray for the Church and for the
world; and let us thank God for his
goodness.
Almighty God, our heavenly Father,
who promised through your Son Jesus
Christ to hear us when we pray in faith:

We give thanks for / we pray for
the Church throughout the world . . .
our own Church, our diocese and bishop . . .
any particular work of the Church . . .

Silence may be kept.

Strengthen your Church to carry forward the work of Christ; that we and all who confess your Name may unite in your truth, live together in your love, and reveal your glory in the world.

Lord, in your mercy

All   **Hear our prayer.**

We give thanks for / we pray for
the nations of the world . . .
our own nation . . .
all men in their various callings . . .

Silence may be kept.

Give wisdom to all in authority, especially Elizabeth our Queen; direct this nation and all nations in the ways of justice and of peace; that men may honour one another, and seek the common good.

Lord, in your mercy

All   **Hear our prayer.**

15

We give thanks for / we pray for
the local community . . .
our families and friends . . .
particular persons . . .

Silence may be kept.

Give grace to us, our families and
friends, and to all our neighbours in
Christ; that we may serve him in one
another, and love as he loves us.

Lord, in your mercy

All   **Hear our prayer.**

We pray for
the sick and the suffering . . .
those who mourn . . .
those without faith . . ,

We give thanks and pray for
all who serve and relieve them . . .

Silence may be kept.

Comfort and heal all those who suffer
in body, mind, or spirit; give them
courage and hope in their troubles; and
bring them the joy of your salvation.

Lord, in your mercy

All   **Hear our prayer.**

16

We commemorate
the departed especially . . .

Silence may be kept.

We commend all men to your unfailing
love, that in them your will may be
fulfilled; and we rejoice at the faithful
witness of your saints in every age,
praying that we may share with them in
your eternal kingdom.

Lord, in your mercy

All **Accept these prayers
for the sake of your Son,
our Saviour Jesus Christ. Amen.**

16 At least on Ash Wednesday and the five Sundays
following, the minister says these commandments;
and silence may be kept after the responses.

Our Lord Jesus Christ said, If you love
me, keep my commandments: happy
are those who hear the word of God
and keep it. Hear then these commandments which God has given to
his people, and take them to heart.
I am the Lord your God: you shall have
no other gods but me.
You shall love the Lord your God with
all your heart, with all your soul, with all
your mind, and with all your strength.

All   **Amen. Lord, have mercy.**

Minister   You shall not make for yourself any idol.
God is spirit, and those who worship
him must worship in spirit and in truth.

All   **Amen. Lord, have mercy.**

Minister   You shall not dishonour the name of
the Lord your God.
You shall worship him with reverence
and awe.

All   **Amen. Lord, have mercy.**

Minister   Remember the Lord's day and keep it
holy.
Christ is risen from the dead; set your
minds on things that are above, not on
things that are on the earth.

All   **Amen. Lord, have mercy.**

Minister	Honour your father and mother. Live as servants of God; honour all men; love the brotherhood.
All	**Amen. Lord, have mercy.**

Minister	You shall not commit murder. Do not nurse anger against your brother; overcome evil with good.
All	**Amen. Lord, have mercy.**

Minister	You shall not commit adultery. Know that your body is a temple of the Holy Spirit.
All	**Amen. Lord, have mercy.**

Minister	You shall not steal. You shall do honest work, that you may be able to give to those in need.
All	**Amen. Lord, have mercy.**

Minister	You shall not be a false witness. Let everyone speak the truth.
All	**Amen. Lord, have mercy.**

Minister	You shall not covet anything which belongs to your neighbour. Remember the words of the Lord Jesus: It is more blessed to give than to receive. Love your neighbour as yourself, for love is the fulfilling of the law.
All	**Amen. Lord, have mercy.**

17 Minister   God so loved the world that he gave his only Son, Jesus Christ, to save us from our sins, to be our advocate in heaven, and to bring us to eternal life.

Let us therefore confess our sins, in penitence and faith, firmly resolved to keep God's commandments and to live in love and peace with all men.

Or he says one or more of these sentences:

Hear the words of comfort our Saviour Christ says to all who truly turn to him.

Come to me, all who labour and are heavy-laden, and I will give you rest.

God so loved the world that he gave his only Son, that whoever believes in him should not perish but have eternal life.

Hear what St Paul says.

This saying is true and worthy of full acceptance, that Christ Jesus came into the world to save sinners.

Hear what St John says.

If anyone does sin, we have an advocate with the Father, Jesus Christ the righteous; and he is the expiation of our sins.

After which he says:

> Let us therefore confess our sins, in penitence and faith, firmly resolved to keep God's commandments and to live in love and peace with all men.

18 Kneel

Silence may be kept.

All
**Father eternal, Giver of light and grace,
we have sinned against you and against
    our fellow men,
in what we have thought,
in what we have said and done,
through ignorance, through weakness,
through our own deliberate fault.
We have wounded your love,
and marred your image in us.
We are sorry and ashamed,
and repent of all our sins.
For the sake of your Son, Jesus Christ,
    who died for us,
forgive us all that is past,
and lead us out from darkness
to walk as children of light. Amen.**

19 Minister
Almighty God, who pardons all who truly repent, have mercy upon you, pardon and deliver you from all your sins, confirm and strengthen you in all goodness, and keep you in life eternal; through Jesus Christ our Lord.

All
Amen.

20 All may say

We do not presume
to come to this your table, merciful Lord,
trusting in our own righteousness,
but in your manifold and great mercies.
We are not worthy
so much as to gather up the crumbs under
    your table.
But you are the same Lord
whose nature is always to have mercy.
Grant us therefore, gracious Lord,
so to eat the flesh of your dear Son Jesus
    Christ,
and to drink his blood,
that we may evermore dwell in him,
and he in us. Amen.

or

Most merciful Lord,
your love compels us to come in.
Our hands were unclean,
our hearts were unprepared;
we were not fit
even to eat the crumbs from under your
    table.
But you, Lord, are the God of our
    salvation,
and share your bread with sinners.
So cleanse and feed us
with the precious body and blood of
    your Son,
that he may live in us and we in him;
and that we, with the whole company
    of Christ,
may sit and eat in your kingdom. Amen.

The Communion

RELIGIOUS EDUCATION ROOM
NOTRE DAME COLLEGE OF EDUCATION 1
MOUNT PLEASANT, LIVERPOOL, 3

The Peace

21 Stand

President   We are the Body of Christ. In the one Spirit we were all baptized into one body. Let us then pursue all that makes for peace and builds up our common life.

22 The president gives the Peace to the congregation, saying

The peace of the Lord be always with you;

All   **And also with you.**

The Taking of the Bread and Wine

23 A hymn may be sung, and the offerings of the people may be collected and presented.

24 The bread and wine are brought to the holy table.

25 The president takes the bread and wine.

The Thanksgiving

26 The president says,

	The Lord is here.
All	**His Spirit is with us.**
President	Lift up your hearts.
All	**We lift them to the Lord.**
President	Let us give thanks to the Lord our God.
All	**It is right to give him thanks and praise.**

27 President   It is not only right, it is our duty and our joy, at all times and in all places, to give you thanks and praise, holy Father, heavenly King, almighty and eternal God, through Jesus Christ, your only Son, our Lord;

For he is your living Word; through him you have created all things from the beginning, and formed us in your own image;

Through him you have freed us from the slavery of sin, giving him to be born as man, to die upon the cross, and to rise again for us;

Through him you have made us a people for your own possession, exalting him to your right hand on high, and sending upon us your holy and life-giving Spirit.

Advent

And now we give you thanks, because the day of our deliverance has dawned; and through him you will make all things new, as he comes in power and triumph to judge the world.

Christmas
Presentation
Annunciation

because by the power of the Holy Spirit he took our nature upon him and was born of the Virgin Mary his mother, that being himself without sin he might make us clean from all sin.

Epiphany
Transfigur-
ation

because in coming to dwell among us as man, he revealed the radiance of his glory, and brought us out of darkness into his own marvellous light.

Lent

because through him you have given us the spirit of discipline, that we may triumph over evil and grow in grace.

Passiontide

because for our salvation he was obedient even to death on the cross. The tree of defeat became the tree of glory; and where life was lost, there life has been restored.

Easter

for his glorious resurrection from the dead. By his death he has destroyed death, and by his rising again he has restored to us eternal life.

Ascension	because in his risen body he appeared to his disciples and in their sight was taken into heaven, to reign with you in glory.
Whitsun	because by that same Spirit we are led into all truth and are given power to proclaim your gospel to the nations and to serve you as a royal priesthood.
Trinity Sunday	because you have revealed your glory as the glory of your Son and of the Holy Spirit: three persons equal in majesty, undivided in splendour, yet one Lord, one God, ever to be worshipped and adored.
Saints' Days	for the glorious pledge of the hope of our calling which you have given us in your saints; that, following their example and strengthened by their fellowship, we may run with perseverance the race that is set before us, and with them receive the unfading crown of glory.
Dedication	for your blessings on this house of prayer, where we are stirred to faithful witness and are built by your Spirit into a temple made without hands, even the body of your Son, Jesus Christ.

29

Therefore with angels and archangels, and with all the company of heaven, we proclaim your great and glorious Name, for ever praising you and saying:

All

Holy, holy, holy Lord,
God of power and might,
Heaven and earth are full of your glory.
Hosanna in the highest.

President

Accept our praises, heavenly Father, through your Son, our Saviour Jesus Christ; and as we follow his example and obey his command, grant that these gifts of bread and wine may be to us his body and his blood;

For in the same night that he was betrayed, he took bread; and after giving you thanks, he broke it, gave it to his disciples, and said, 'Take, eat; this is my body which I give for you. Do this in remembrance of me.' Again, after supper he took the cup; he gave you thanks, and gave it to them, saying, 'Drink this, all of you; for this is my blood of the new Covenant, which I shed for you and for many, for the forgiveness of sins. Do this, as often as you drink it, in remembrance of me.'

All   **Christ has died:**
Christ is risen:
In Christ shall all be made alive.

President   Therefore, heavenly Father, we do this
in remembrance of him: with this bread
and this cup we celebrate his perfect
sacrifice made once for all upon the
cross; we proclaim his resurrection
from the dead and his ascension into
heaven; and we look for the fullness of
his coming in glory. Accept this our
sacrifice of thanks and praise; and as
we eat and drink these holy gifts in the
presence of your divine majesty, renew
us by your Spirit, inspire us with your
love, and unite us in the body of your
Son, Jesus Christ our Lord.

With him, and in him, and through him,
by the power of the Holy Spirit, with
all who stand before you in earth and
heaven, we worship you, Father
Almighty, in songs of everlasting praise:

All   **Blessing and honour and glory and power
be yours for ever and ever. Amen.**

Silence may be kept.

The Breaking of the Bread

30 The president breaks the consecrated bread, saying:

> We break this bread
> to share in the body of Christ.

All **Though we are many, we are one body,
because we all share in one bread.**

The Giving of the Bread and the Cup

31 President As our Saviour has taught us,
so we pray:

All **Our Father in heaven,
holy be your Name,
your kingdom come,
your will be done,
on earth as in heaven.
Give us today our daily bread.
Forgive us our sins
as we forgive those who sin against us.
Do not bring us to the test
but deliver us from evil.**

**For the kingdom, the power and the glory
  are yours
now and for ever. Amen.**

32 President   Draw near with faith. Receive the body
of our Lord Jesus Christ which he gave
for you, and his blood which he shed
for you. Remember that he died for you,
and feed on him in your hearts by faith
with thanksgiving.

33 The president and the other communicants receive the
holy communion.

At the administration the ministers say to each
communicant

> The Body of Christ keep you
> in eternal life.

> The Blood of Christ keep you
> in eternal life.

The communicant replies each time,

Amen.

and then receives.

34 During THE COMMUNION these and other hymns
and anthems may be sung:

> **Blessed is he who comes in the name**
> **of the Lord. Hosanna in the highest.**

> **Jesus, Lamb of God: have mercy on us.**
> **Jesus, bearer of our sins: have mercy**
> **on us.**
> **Jesus, redeemer of the world: give us**
> **your peace.**

35 If either or both of the consecrated elements are likely
to prove insufficient, the president returns to the holy
table and adds more, either in silence or with these
words:

> Having given thanks to you, Father,
> over the bread and the cup as your Son
> our Lord Jesus Christ commanded, we
> receive this bread/wine also as his
> body/blood.

36 Any consecrated bread and wine which is not required
for purposes of communion is consumed at the end of
the administration, or after the service.

After Communion

37 A seasonal sentence may be said.

Advent   Our Lord says, 'Surely I come quickly.'
Even so: come, Lord Jesus!

Christmas   The bread of God is he who comes
down from heaven and gives life to
the world.

Lent   Jesus said, 'You are those who have
continued with me in my trials; you
shall eat and drink at my table in
my kingdom.'

Passiontide   As we eat this bread and drink this cup,
we proclaim the death of the Lord until
he comes.

Easter	Jesus said, 'He who eats my flesh and drinks my blood has eternal life, and I will raise him up at the last day.'
Ascension	God has highly exalted his Son, and given him a name which is above all other names, that at the name of Jesus every knee shall bow.
Whitsun	God who raised Christ Jesus from the dead will also give life to your mortal bodies through his Spirit who dwells in you.
Trinity Sunday	We were chosen of old in the purpose of the Father, hallowed to his service in the Spirit, and consecrated with the blood of Jesus Christ.
Saints' Days	You have come to Mount Zion, to God the judge of all, to the spirits of just men made perfect, and to Jesus the mediator of the new covenant.
Dedication	The heaven of heavens cannot contain our God; how much less this house that we have built!
Unity	Through Christ Jesus we all have access to the Father in the one Spirit.

Silence may be kept.

33

Father of all, we give you thanks and praise, that when we were still far off you met us in your Son and brought us home. Dying and living, he declared your love, gave us grace, and opened the gate of glory. May we who share Christ's body live his risen life; we who drink his cup bring life to others; we whom the Spirit lights give light to the world. Anchor us in this hope that we have grasped; so we and all your children shall be free, and the whole earth live to praise your Name; through Christ our Lord.

All   **Amen.**

39 All   **Almighty God,**
we thank you for feeding us
with the body and blood of your Son
**   Jesus Christ.**
Through him we offer you
**   our souls and bodies**
to be a living sacrifice.
Send us out
in the power of your Spirit
to live and work
to your praise and glory. Amen.

40 A hymn or canticle may be sung.

41 The president may say this or the appropriate seasonal blessing.

> The peace of God, which passes all understanding, keep your hearts and minds in the knowledge and love of God, and of his Son Jesus Christ our Lord;

> And the blessing of God Almighty, the Father, the Son, and the Holy Spirit, be among you, and remain with you always.

All　　**Amen.**

42 President　　Go in peace and serve the Lord.

All　　**In the name of Christ. Amen.**

43 The Ministers and people depart.

44 Seasonal Blessings

Advent　　The Sun of righteousness shine upon you and scatter the darkness from before your path; and the blessing...

Christmas　　Christ the Son of God gladden your hearts with the good news of his kingdom; and the blessing...

Lent　　Christ bestow upon you the spirit of holy discipline to deny yourself, take up your cross, and follow him; and the blessing...

Passiontide　　Christ the Saviour draw you to himself, so that you find in him crucified a sure ground for faith, a firm support for hope, and the assurance of sins forgiven; and the blessing...

Easter The God of peace, who brought again from the dead our Lord Jesus, that great shepherd of the sheep, through the blood of the everlasting covenant, make you perfect in every good work to do his will, working in you that which is well-pleasing in his sight; and the blessing...

Ascension Christ our king make you faithful and patient to do his will, that you may reign with him in glory; and the blessing...

Whitsun The Spirit of truth lead you into all truth, give you grace to confess that Jesus Christ is Lord, and to proclaim the word and works of God; and the blessing...

Trinity Sunday God the Holy Trinity make you strong in faith and love, defend you on every side, and guide you in truth and peace; and the blessing...

Saints' Days God give you grace to follow his saints in faith and hope and love; and the blessing...

Unity Christ the good shepherd bring you and all who hear his voice to be one flock, gathered into one fold; and the blessing...

Appendix

Tables of Psalms and Lessons

The psalms and lessons in these tables following are to
be used at Holy Communion in accordance with the
Rules to Order the Service.* The numbering of the verses
of the psalms is according to the Revised Psalter. A
different numbering in the Prayer Book version is
indicated in square brackets. Other references to
passages of scripture are to the Revised Standard
Version; but any version of holy scripture may be used
which is permitted by lawful authority.

* Now awaiting consideration by the General Synod.

Table 1

The psalms and lessons in this table are appointed for use on Sundays and certain other days, and may also be used on the weekdays which follow.

They may also be used at Morning and Evening Prayer on their appointed days. At Holy Communion on weekdays the lessons of the Alternative Lectionary (1970) may also be used, in such a way that when the lessons for one year are read at Morning and Evening Prayer, the lessons for the alternate year are read at Holy Communion.

Note that the lessons for the five Sundays before Advent Sunday shall always be those provided for Trinity 23 and the four weeks following. Lessons for Trinity 18 to Trinity 22 will be used according as they are needed.

	Year 1	**Year 2**
Advent 1	Psalm 50.1–6/Psalm 82	
	Isa. 52.1–10	Isa. 51.4–11
	1 Thess. 5.1–11	Rom. 13.8–14
	Luke 21.25–33	Matt. 25.31–46
Advent 2	Psalm 19.7–11/Psalm 119.129–136	
	Isa. 55.1–11 (–13)	Isa. 64.1–5 (–12)
	Rom. 15.4–13	2 Tim. 3.14—4.5
	John 5.36–47	Luke 4.14–21

Advent 3	Psalm 126/Benedictus	
	Isa. 40.1–11	Mal. 3.1–5
		or 3.1–5, 4.1
	1 Cor. 4.1–5	Phil. 4.4–9
	John 1.19–27	Matt. 11.2–15
Advent 4	Psalm 45.10–17/Magnificat	
	Isa. 11.1–9	Zech. 2.10–13
	1 Cor. 1.26–31	Rev. 21.1–7
	Luke 1.26–38a	Matt. 1.18–23
Christmas Day	Psalm 85.8–13/Psalm 98	
	Micah 5.2–4 *or*	Isa. 9.2–7
	Titus 2.11–14	1 John 4.7–14
	Luke 2.1–20	John 1.1–14
Christmas 1	Psalm 66.1–7/Psalm 72.7–14	
	Isa. 60.1–6 (–22)	Isa. 49.7–13
		(1–13)
	Heb. 1.1–4	Eph. 3.1–6
	Matt. 2.1–12	Matt. 2.1–12
Christmas 2	Psalm 116.11–16/Nunc Dimittis	
	1 Sam. 1.20–28	Deut. 16.1–6
	(1–28)	
	Rom. 12.1–8	Rom. 8.12–17
	Luke 2.21–40	Luke 2.41–52
Epiphany 1	Psalm 36.5–10/Psalm 89.19–29	
	[20–30]	
	1 Sam. 16.1–13a	Isa. 42.1–7 (–12)
	Acts 10.34–48a	Eph. 2.1–10
	Matt. 3.13–17	John 1.29–34

Epiphany 2	Psalm 100/Psalm 145.1–12
	Jer. 1.4–10 (–19) 1 Sam. 3.1–10
	(–20)
	Acts 26.1, 9–18 Gal. 1.11–24
	Mark 1.14–20 John 1.35–51

Epiphany 2
Psalm 100/Psalm 145.1–12
Jer. 1.4–10 (–19)   1 Sam. 3.1–10
                 (–20)
Acts 26.1, 9–18   Gal. 1.11–24
Mark 1.14–20   John 1.35–51

Epiphany 3
Psalm 84.1–8 [1–7]/Psalm 67
Exod. 33.12–23   1 Kings 8.22–30
(7–23)
1 John 1.1–4   1 Cor. 3.10–17
John 2.1–11   John 2.13–22

Epiphany 4
Psalm 103.1–13/Psalm 85.1–7
Hos. 14.1–7   1 Kings 10.1–13
Philem. 1–16   Eph. 3.8–19
Mark 2.13–17   John 4.7–14

Epiphany 5
Psalm 138/Psalm 31.21–27
Joel 2.15–19,   Lam. 3.19–26
21–22
2 Cor. 3.4–11   1 Thess. 5.12–24
Mark 2.18–22   Matt. 20.1–15

Epiphany 6
Psalm 43/Psalm 51.10–17
Isa. 1.10–17   Exod. 19.16–24
1 Cor. 3.18–23   Heb. 12.18–29
Mark 2.23—3.6   John 4.19–26

Septuagesima
Psalm 103.1–9/Psalm 34.11–18
Isa. 30.18–21   Prov. 3.1–8 (–18)
(8–21)
1 Cor. 4.8–13   1 Cor. 2.1–10
Matt. 5.1–12   Luke 8.4–15

40

Sexagesima	Psalm 48.9–14 [8–13]/Psalm 131
	Zeph. 3.14–20	2 Kings 5.1–14
		(–27)
	Jas. 5.13–16	2 Cor. 12.1–10
	Mark 2.1–12	Mark 1.35–45

Quinquagesima	Psalm 46/Psalm 107.1–9
	Deut. 8.1–6 (–10)	Jonah 1.1–17
	Phil. 4.10–20	Jas. 1.2–12
	John 6.1–14	Mark 4.35–41

Ash	Psalm 90.1–12/Psalm 51.1–17
Wednesday	
	Isa. 58.1–8 (–12)	Amos 5.6–15
		(4–15)
	1 Cor. 9.24–27	Jas. 4.1–8a
	Matt. 6.16–21	Luke 18.9–14

Lent 1	Psalm 119.1–8/Psalm 15
	Deut. 30.15–20	Deut. 6.10–17
	(11–20)	
	Heb. 2.14–18	Heb. 4.12–16
	Matt. 4.1–17	Luke 4.1–13

Lent 2	Psalm 119.33–40/Psalm 18.17–25
	[16–24]	
	2 Kings 6.8–17	Isa. 35.1–10
	(–23)	
	1 John 4.1–6	1 John 3.1–8
	Luke 11.14–26	Matt. 12.22–32

Lent 3	Psalm 119.105–112/Psalm 115.1–8
	Isa. 59.12–20	Isa. 45.18–25
	(1–21)	(14–25)
	1 Pet. 2.19–25	Col. 1.24–29
	Matt. 16.13–28	Luke 9.18–27

Lent 4	Psalm 119.153–160/Psalm 18.26–37
	[25–36]
	Exod. 34.29–35	1 Kings 19.1–12
		(–18)
	2 Cor. 3.12–18	2 Pet. 1.16–19
	Matt. 17.1–13	Luke 9.28–36

Lent 5	Psalm 76.1–9/Psalm 22.22–28
	Isa. 63.1–9 (–16)	Jer. 31.31–34
	Col. 2.8–15	Heb. 9.11–15
	John 12.20–32	Mark 10.32–45

Palm Sunday	Psalm 24/Psalm 45.1–7
	Zech. 9.9–12	Isa. 52.13–53.12
	1 Cor. 1.18–25	Heb. 10.1–10
	Matt. 21.1–11	Matt. 21.1–11
	or 26.1—27.61	*or* 26.1—27.61
	or 27.1–61	*or* 27.1–61

Monday	Psalm 130/Psalm 79.8–10
before Easter	Isa. 42.1–4	Lam. 3.19–33
	Acts 10.34–43	Phil. 2.1–13
	Mark 14.1–26	Luke 22.1–38

Tuesday	Psalm 69.17–23 [17–22]/Psalm
before Easter	35.11–16
	Isa. 49.1–6	Gen. 22.1–12
	Heb. 4.14—5.10	Col. 2.6–15
	Mark 14.27–72	Luke 22.39–71

Wednesday	Psalm 102.1–11/Psalm 55.12–15	
before Easter	Isa. 50.4–9	Num. 21.4–9
	1 Pet. 2.18–25	1 Cor. 1.18–25
	Mark 15.1–41	Luke 23.1–47

Maundy	Psalm 116.11–16/Psalm 41	
Thursday	Isa. 52.13—53.12	Jer. 31.31–34
	1 Cor. 11.23–29	1 Cor. 10.16–17
	John 13.1–15	Mark 14.12–26

Good Friday Psalm 88.1–13/Psalm 54
Exod. 12.1–8, 11
Heb. 10.11–25
John 18.1—19.37 *or* 19.1–37

Easter Eve Psalm 16.9–12/Psalm 139.6–11
Hag. 2.6–9
1 Pet. 3.17–22
Matt. 27.57–66 *or* John 2.18–22

Easter Day (i) Easter Anthems/Psalm 118.15–24
(ii) Psalm 114/Te Deum, part 2

Isa. 12.1–6	Isa. 12.1–6
Rev. 1.12–18	1 Cor. 5.7b–8
Mark 16.1–8	Matt. 28.1–10

or in either year:
Exod. 14.15–22 (5–30a)
1 Cor. 15.12–20
John 20.1–18

Easter 1	Psalm 145.1–7/Psalm 68.1–8	
	Exod. 15.1–11	Exod. 16.4–15
	(–18)	(1–15, 31–35)
	1 Pet. 1.3–9	1 Cor. 15.53–58
	John 20.19–29	John 6.35–40
Easter 2	Psalm 111/Psalm 23	
	Isa. 25.6–9 (1–9)	Ezek. 34.7–15
		(1–15)
	Rev. 19.6–9	1 Pet. 5.1–11
	Luke 24.13–35	John 10.7–18
Easter 3	Psalm 16.6–12/Psalm 30.1–6	
	Isa. 61.1–3 (–11)	1 Kings 17.17–24
		(8–24)
	1 Cor. 15.1–11	Col. 3.1–11
	John 21.1–14	John 11.17–27
Easter 4	Psalm 33.1–8/Psalm 37.23–32	
	Isa. 62.1–5 (–12)	Prov. 4.10–18
		(1–18)
	Rev. 3.14–22	2 Cor. 4.11–18
	John 21.15–22	John 14.1–11
Easter 5	Psalm 84.1–6 [1–5]/Psalm 15	
	Isa. 51.1–6 (–16)	Deut. 34.1–12
	1 Cor. 15.21–28	Rom. 8.28–39
	John 16.25–33	John 16.12–24
Ascension Day	Psalm 8/Psalm 21.1–6	
	Dan. 7.13–14	
	Acts 1.1–11	
	Matt. 28.16–20	

Sunday after *Ascension Day*	Psalm 24/Psalm 47	
	Dan. 7.9–14	2 Kings 2.1–15
	Eph. 1.15–23	Eph. 4.1–8, 11–13
	Luke 24.44–53	Luke 24.44–53

Whitsunday	Psalm 122/Psalm 36.5–10	
	Joel 2.23–29	Joel 2.28–32
	(21–32)	(21–32)
	Acts 2.1–11	Acts 2.1–11
	John 14.15–27	John 14.15–27

Trinity Sunday	Psalm 93/Psalm 97. 1–9	
	Isa. 6.1–8	Deut. 6.4–9
	Eph. 1.3–14	Acts 2.22–24, 32–36
	John 14.8–17	Matt. 11.25–30

Trinity 1	Psalm 95.1–7/Psalm 135.1–6	
	Exod. 19.1–6	2 Sam. 7.4–16
	(–11)	(1–17)
	1 Pet. 2.1–10	Acts 2.37–47
	John 15.1–5	Luke 14.15–24

Trinity 2	Psalm 84.1–8 [1–7]/Psalm 139.1–11	
	Deut. 6.17–25	Deut. 8.11–20
	Rom. 6.1–11	Acts 4.5–12
	John 15.6–11	Luke 8.41–55

Trinity 3	Psalm 63.1–9/Psalm 67	
	Deut. 7.6–9a	Josh. 24.14–25
	(1–11)	(1–5, 14–28)
	Gal. 3.26—4.7	Acts 8.26–38
	John 15.12–15	Luke 15.1–10

Trinity 4	Psalm 119.57–64/Psalm 119.89–96	
	Exod. 20.1–17	Ruth 1.8–17, 22
		(1–22)
	Eph. 5.1–10	Acts 11.4–18
	Matt. 19.16–26	Luke 17.11–19

Trinity 5	Psalm 112/Psalm 1	
	Exod. 24.3–11	Mic. 6.1–8
	(1–18)	
	Col. 3.12–17	Eph. 4.17–32
	Luke 15.11–32	Mark 10.46–52

Trinity 6	Psalm 62.1–8/Psalm 103.8–18	
	Hos. 11.1–9	Deut. 10.12—11.1
	1 Cor. 13.1–13	Rom. 8.1–11
	Matt. 18.21–35	Mark 12.28–34

Trinity 7	Psalm 25.1–9/Psalm 26.1–8	
	Ezek. 36.24–28	Ezek. 37.1–14
	(22–32)	
	Gal. 5.16–25	1 Cor. 12.4–13
	John 15.16–27	Luke 6.27–38

Trinity 8	Psalm 18.1–7 [1–6]/Psalm 18.32–37	
	[31–36]	
	Josh. 1.1–9	1 Sam. 17.37–50
		(1–11, 32–50)
	Eph. 6.10–18a	2 Cor. 6.3–10
	John 17.11–19	Mark 9.14–29

Trinity 9	Psalm 71.1–8 [1–7]/Psalm 73.23–28 [22–27]	
	Job. 42.1–6 (38.1–11, 42.1–6)	1 Sam. 24.9–17 (1–17)
	Phil. 2.1–13	Gal. 6.1–10
	John 13.1–15	Luke 7.36–50

Trinity 10	Psalm 123/Psalm 31.21–27	
	Isa. 42.1–7 (–12)	1 Chron. 29.1–9 (–16)
	2 Cor. 4.1–10	Phil. 1.1–11
	John 13.33–36	Luke 17.5–10

Trinity 11	Psalm 96.1–6/Psalm 96.7–13	
	Isa. 49.1–6 (–13)	Mic. 4.1–7
	2 Cor. 5.14—6.2	Acts 17.22–31
	John 17.20–26	Matt. 5.13–16

Trinity 12	Psalm 31.1–6/Psalm 43	
	Isa. 50.4–9 (–11)	Jer. 12.1–6 (11.18–20, 12.1–6)
	1 Pet. 4.12–19	Acts 20.17–35
	John 16.1–11	Matt. 10.16–22

Trinity 13	Psalm 34.1–10/Psalm 34.11–18	
	Lev. 19.9–18 (1–4, 9–18)	Deut. 15.7–11 (1–18)
	Rom. 12.9–21	1 John 4.15–21
	Luke 10.25–37	Luke 16.19–31

Trinity 14	Psalm 127/Psalm 128	
	Isa. 54.1–8 (–17)	Gen. 45.1–15
		(–28)
	Eph. 5.21—6.4	1 Pet. 3.1–9
	Mark 10.2–16	Luke 14.25–33

Trinity 15	Psalm 72.1–8/Psalm 20	
	Isa. 45.1–7 (–13)	1 Kings 3.5–15
	Rom. 13.1–7	1 Tim. 2.1–7
	Matt. 22.15–22	Luke 11.1–13

Trinity 16	Psalm 56/Psalm 57	
	Jer. 7.1–7 (–14)	Jer. 32.6–15
		(1–15)
	Jas. 1.22–27	Gal. 2.20—3.9
	Matt. 7.21–29	Luke 7.1–10

Trinity 17	Psalm 145.9–16/Psalm 90.13–17	
	Deut. 26.1–11	Ecclus. 38.24–34
	(1–11, 16–19)	*or* Neh. 6.1–16
	2 Cor. 8.1–9	1 Pet. 4.7–11
	Matt. 5.21–26	Matt. 25.14–29

Trinity 18	Psalm 139.1–9/Psalm 71.1–8 [1–7]	
	Gen. 28.10–22	Dan. 6.10–23
		(1–23)
	Heb. 11.1–3, 7–16	Rom. 5.1–11
	Luke 5.1–11	Luke 19.1–10

Trinity 19	Psalm 15/Psalm 146.5–10 [4–10]
	Jer. 29.1, 4–14 Isa. 33.17–22
	(13–22)
	Phil. 3.7–21 Rev. 7.9–17
	John 17.1–10 Matt. 25.1–13
Trinity 20	Psalm 37.1–11/Psalm 121
	Dan. 3.13–25 Gen. 32.24–30
	(1–25) (1–30)
	Heb. 11.32—12.2 1 Cor. 9.19–27
	Luke 9.51–62 Matt. 7.13–20
Trinity 21	Psalm 43/Psalm 51.10–17
	Exod. 19.16–24 Isa. 1.10–17
	Heb. 12.18–29 1 Cor. 3.18–23
	John 4.19–26 Mark 2.23—3.6
Trinity 22	Psalm 138/Psalm 31.21–27
	Lam. 3.19–26 Joel 2.15–19,
	21–22
	1 Thess. 5.12–24 2 Cor. 3.4–11
	Matt. 20.1–15 Mark 2.18–22
Trinity 23:	Psalm 104.1–9/Psalm 104.25–31
Fifth Sunday	[24–30]
before Advent	Gen. 1.1–3, Gen. 2.4b–9,
	24–31a (1.1—2.3) 15–25
	Col. 1.15–20 Rev. 4.1–11
	John 1.1–14 John 3.1–8

Trinity 24:	Psalm 130/Psalm 10.13–20	
Fourth Sunday	Gen. 3.1–15	Gen. 4.1–10
before Advent	(–24)	(–16)
	Rom. 7.7–12	1 John 3.9–18
	John 3.13–21	Mark 7.14–23

Trinity 25:	Psalm 1/Psalm 105.1–11	
Third Sunday	Gen. 12.1–9	Gen. 22.1–18
before Advent	Rom. 4.13–25	Jas. 2.14–24
	John 8.51–58	Luke 20.9–16

Trinity 26:	Psalm 135.1–6/Psalm 77.11–20	
Second Sunday	Exod. 3.1–15	Exod. 6.2–8
before Advent	(–22)	(–13)
	Heb. 3.1–6	Heb. 11.17–29
	John 6.27–35	Mark 13.5–13

Trinity 27:	Psalm 80.1–7/Psalm 80.8–19	
Sunday next	1 Kings 19.9–18	Isa. 10.20–23
before Advent	Rom. 11.13–24	Rom. 9.19–29
	Matt. 24.38–44	Mark 13.14–23

Table 2

| *The Circumcision of Christ*, or *The Naming of Jesus*
 January 1 | Psalm 8/Psalm 62.1–8
 Isa. 9.6–7
 Acts 4.8–12
 Luke 2.15–21 |

The Circumcision of
Christ, or The Naming
of Jesus
January 1

Psalm 8/Psalm 62.1–8
Isa. 9.6–7
Acts 4.8–12
Luke 2.15–21

The Epiphany, or The
Manifestation of
Christ to the
Gentiles
January 6

Psalm 72.1–7/Psalm 72.8–11
Isa. 60.1–6 or 49.7–13
Rev. 21.22—22.5 or Eph. 3.1–12
Matt. 2.1–12 or John 1.14–18

The Conversion of
St Paul
January 25

Psalm 126/Psalm 67
Jer. 1.4–10
Acts 9.1–22
Matt. 19.27–30

The Presentation of
Christ in the Temple,
or The Purification of
St Mary the Virgin
February 2

Psalm 48.1–8 [1–7]/
   Psalm 48.9–14 [8–13]
Mal. 3.1–4
1 Pet. 2.4–10
Luke 2.22–35

St Matthias the
Apostle
February 24

Psalm 16.1–7/Psalm 80.8–15
1 Sam. 2.27–35
Acts 1.15–17, 20–26
John 15.1–10

The Annunciation of the Blessed Virgin Mary *March 25*	Psalm 113/Psalm 131 Gen. 3.8–15 Gal. 4.1–7 Luke 1.26–38a
St Mark the Evangelist *April 25*	Psalm 45.1–4 [1–5]/ Psalm 119.9–16 Prov. 15.28–33 2 Tim. 4.5–11 Mark 13.5–11
St Philip and St James, Apostles *May 1*	Psalm 33.1–6/Psalm 25.1–9 Prov. 4.10–18 Eph. 1.3–10 John 14.1–14
St Barnabas the Apostle *June 11*	Psalm 145.8–15/Psalm 112 Job. 29.11–16 Acts 11.19–26 John 15.12–17
The Nativity of St John Baptist *June 24*	Psalm 119.161–168/ Psalm 80.1–7 Isa. 40.1–5 Gal. 3.23–29 Luke 1.57–66, 80
St Peter the Apostle *June 29*	Psalm 125/Psalm 18.32–36 [31–35] Ezek. 3.4–11 1 Pet. 2.18–25 Matt. 16.13–20

The Visitation of the Blessed Virgin Mary July 2	Psalm 113/Psalm 131 Zech. 2.10–13 Gal. 4.1–5 Luke 1.39–49
St Mary Magdalen July 22	Psalm 139.1–11/ Psalm 30.1–5 Zeph. 3.14–20 2 Cor. 5.14–17 John 20.11–18
St James the Apostle July 25	Psalm 15/Psalm 75.7–12 Jer. 45 Acts 11.27—12.2 Mark 10.35–45
The Transfiguration of our Lord August 6	Psalm 84.1–8 [1–7]/ Psalm 84.9–14 [8–13] Exod. 34.29–35 2 Cor. 3.12–18 Luke 9.28–36
St Bartholomew the Apostle August 24	Psalm 116.11–16/ Psalm 97.10–12 Isa. 61.4–9 Acts 5.12–16 Luke 22.24–30
The Beheading of St John Baptist August 29	Psalm 119.41–48/ Psalm 119.161–168 2 Chron. 24.17–21 Heb. 11.32–40 Matt. 14.1–12

The Nativity of the Blessed Virgin Mary *September 8*	Psalm 113/Psalm 131 Gen. 3.8–15 Gal. 4.1–5 *or* Rom. 5.12–15 Luke 11.27–28 *or* 1.26–38a
St Matthew the Apostle September 21	Psalm 119.65–72/ Psalm 119.89–96 Prov. 3.13–17 2 Cor. 4.1–6 Matt. 9.9–13
St Michael and All Angels September 29	Psalm 103.17–22/ Psalm 91.5–12 2 Kings 6.11–17 Rev. 12.7–12a Matt. 18.1–6, 10
St Luke the Evangelist October 18	Psalm 147.1–6/ Psalm 22.22–28 Isa. 35.3–6 Acts 16.6–12a Luke 10.1–9
St Simon and St Jude, Apostles October 28	Psalm 15/Psalm 116.11–16 Isa. 28.9–16 Eph. 2.13–22 John 15.18–27
All Saints November 1	Psalm 33.1–5/Psalm 145.8–13 Jer. 31.31–34 *or* Gen. 3.1–15 Rev. 7.9–14 Matt. 5.1–12

St Andrew *the Apostle* *November 30*	Psalm 92.1–5/Psalm 87 Zech. 8.20–23 Rom. 10.12–15 Matt. 4.12–20
St Thomas *the Apostle* *December 21*	Psalm 139.1–11/Psalm 31.1–6 Gen. 12.1–5a Heb. 10.35—11.1 John 20.24–29
St Stephen *December 26*	Psalm 119.17–24/ Psalm 119.161–168 2 Chron. 24.20–22 Acts 7.54–60 Luke 11.49–51
St John the *Evangelist* *December 27*	Psalm 117/Psalm 92.12–15 [11–14] Exod. 33.17–23 1 John 2.1–17 John 21.20–25
The Innocents *December 28*	Psalm 123/Psalm 131 Jer. 31.15–17 1 Cor. 1.26–29 Matt. 2.13–18

Table 3

Of a Martyr or
Martyrs

Psalm 119.161–168/
   Psalm 18.32–37 [31–36]
Wisd. 3.1–9
Rom. 8.35–39 *or* Rev. 7.13–17
Matt. 10.16–22 *or* 16.24–26

Of a Doctor or
Confessor

Psalm 119.97–104/
   Psalm 34.11–17
Ecclus. 39.1–10
1 Cor. 2.6–12 *or* 2 Tim. 4.1–8
Matt. 13.51–52 *or* John
   16.12–15

Of a Bishop

Psalm 80.1–7/Psalm 99
Ezek. 34.11–15
1 Pet. 5.1–4 *or* Eph. 4.7–8,
   11–16
John 10.10b–15 *or* 21.15–17

Of an Abbot or Abbess

Psalm 123/Psalm 119.57–64
Jer. 17.7–10
Phil. 3.7–14 *or* 1 John 2.15–17
Matt. 19.23–30 *or* Luke
   12.32–37

Of Missionaries	Psalm 96.1–6/Psalm 96.7–13 Isa. 61.1–3 2 Cor. 4.5–10 *or* Eph. 2.13–22 Matt. 9.35–38 *or* 28.16–20

Of Saints, Martyrs,
Missionaries, and
Doctors of the
Church of England
	Psalm 87/Psalm 67
	Ecclus. 44.1–15 *or* 2.10–18
	Heb. 13.7–8, 15–16
	    or 2 Cor. 4.5–12
	    or Heb. 11.32—12.2
	John 12.20–26 *or* 17.18–23
	    or 15.16–27

Of any Saint	Psalm 119.1–8/
	    Psalm 18.26–31 [25–30]
	Ecclus. 2.1–9
	1 Tim. 6.11–16 *or* Heb. 11.32
	    —12.2
	Matt. 5.13–16 *or* Mark
	    10.42–45

Commemoration of the Faithful Departed and at a Funeral	Collect: Merciful God, Father of our Lord Jesus Christ, who is the resurrection and the life of all the faithful : raise us from the death of sin to the life of righteousness, that at the last we may share with our *brother N.* in your eternal joy; through Jesus Christ our Lord.

Psalm 42.1–7/Psalm 31.21–27
Wisd. 3.1–5, 9
1 Pet. 1.3–9
John 20.1–9 |
| *Ember Days* | Psalm 122/Psalm 84.9–14 [8–13] |
| *1 Lent and Trinity* | Num. 11.16–17, 24–29
Acts 20.28–35
Luke 4.16–21 |
| *2 Michaelmas* | Num. 27.15–23
1 Cor. 3.5–11
John 4.31–38 |
| *3 Advent* | Jer. 1.4–10
1 Pet. 4.7–11
Luke 12.35–43 |

Rogation Days	Psalm 34.1–10/Psalm 121
	Deut. 8.1–10 *or* Joel 2.21–27
	   or Job 28.1–11
	Jas. 5.7–11 *or* Phil. 4.4–7
	   or 2 Thess. 3.6–13
	Luke 11.5–13 *or* Matt. 6.1–15
	   or Luke 5.1–11

Feast of the Dedication or Consecration of a Church	Psalm 84.1–8 [1–7]/
	   Psalm 122 (other Psalms: 24,
	   103, 132)
	1 Kings 8.22–30
	1 Pet. 2.1–5
	Matt. 21.12–16

Patronal Feast of a Church	Unless other provision is made, the appropriate group of lessons from the above list may be used. These may also be used for memorial services or on other occasions.

Thanksgiving for
Harvest

Psalm 104.20–29 [19–28]/
    Psalm 65 (other Psalms: 67,
    145, 147, 148, 150)
Deut. 8.3–10 *or* Gen. 1.24–31a
1 Tim. 6.6–10 *or* Acts 14.13–17
John 6.27–35 *or* Luke
    12.16–31

(Other Lessons:
Gen. 1.1—2.3; Deut. 26.1–11;
    Deut. 28.1–14
Acts 10.10–16; 2 Cor. 9.6–15;
    Rev. 14.14–18
Matt. 6.24–34; Matt. 13.18–30;
    John 4.31–38)

Thanksgiving for the Institution of Holy Baptism

Collect: Almighty God our heavenly Father, who hast given us the sacrament of holy baptism that souls being born again may be made heirs of everlasting salvation: we yield thee thanks for this gift, and beseech thee to grant that we who have been made partakers of the death of thy Son may also share in his resurrection; through the same Jesus Christ our Lord.

Psalm 42.1–7/Psalm 34.1–8
Ezek. 36.25–28
Rom. 6.3–4
Matt. 28.18–20

Thanksgiving for the Institution of Holy Communion

Psalm 43/Psalm 116.11–16
Exod. 16.2–15
1 Cor. 11.23–28
John 6.53–58

For the Missionary Work of the Church Overseas

Psalm 97/Psalm 100 (other Psalms: 2, 46, 47, 67, 72, 87, 96, 117)
Isa. 49.1–6
Eph. 2.13–22
Matt. 28.16–20

For the Guidance of the Holy Spirit	Psalm 25.1–9/ Psalm 143.8–11 [8–10] Wisd. 9.13–17 1 Cor. 12.4–13 John 14.23–26
For the Peace of the World	Psalm 72.1–7/Psalm 85.8–13 Mic. 4.3–5 1 Tim. 2.1–5 Matt. 5.43–48
For the Unity of the Church	Psalm 133/Psalm 122 Jer. 33.6–9a Eph. 4.1–6 John 17.11b–23
In Time of Trouble	Collect: Almighty and ever-lasting God, mercifully look upon our infirmities, and in all our dangers and necessities stretch forth thy right hand to help and defend us; through Jesus Christ our Lord. Psalm 86.1–7/Psalm 142.1–7 Job 1.13–22 *or* Gen. 9.8–17 Rom. 3.21–26 *or* 8.18–25 Luke 12.1–7 *or* Mark 11.22–26

At a Marriage

Collect: O God our Father, you have taught us by your holy apostle that love is the fulfilling of the law; grant to these your servants that, loving one another, they may continue in your love until their lives' end; through Jesus Christ our Lord.

Psalm 67/Psalm 128 (other
    Psalms 23, 37.3–7, 121)
Gen. 2.18, 21–24
Col. 3. 12–17
John 15.9–12 *or* Matt. 7.24–29

First published in 1971
Second impression 1971
SPCK Holy Trinity Church
Marylebone Road, London NW1 4DU

Printed in Great Britain by
William Clowes & Sons, Limited
London, Beccles and Colchester

Designed by Keith Murgatroyd PSTD, FSIA

© The Registrars of the Provinces of Canterbury and York, 1971

Biblical quotations from the *Revised Standard Version* of the
Bible, copyrighted 1946 and 1952 by the Division of
Christian Education of the National Council of the Churches
of Christ in the United States of America; from the *New
English Bible,* copyrighted 1961 and 1970 by Oxford and
Cambridge University Presses; and from the *Jerusalem Bible,*
copyrighted 1966 and 1967 by Darton, Longman & Todd Ltd
and Doubleday and Company Inc., are used by permission.

SBN 281 02658 0